SUPER-EASY
STEP-BY-STEP
CHEESEMAKING

Other Books by Yvonne Young Tarr

The Ten Minute Gourmet Cookbook
The Ten Minute Gourmet Diet Cookbook
101 Desserts to Make You Famous
Love Portions
The New York Times Natural Foods Dieting Book
The Complete Outdoor Cookbook
The New York Times Bread and Soup Cookbook
The Farmhouse Cookbook
Super-Easy Step-by-Step Winemaking
Super-Easy Step-by-Step Sausagemaking
Super-Easy Step-by-Step Book of Special Breads
The Up-with-Wholesome, Down-with-Storebought Book of
Recipes and Household Formulas

SUPER-EASY
STEP-BY-STEP
CHEESEMAKING

YVONNE YOUNG TARR

Vintage Books
A Division of Random House, Inc.
New York

VINTAGE BOOKS EDITION 1975

Copyright © 1975 by Yvonne Young Tarr

All rights reserved under International and
Pan-American Copyright Conventions.
Published in the United States by Random
House, Inc., New York, and simultaneously
in Canada by Random House of Canada
Limited, Toronto.

Library of Congress Cataloging in Publication Data

Tarr, Yvonne Young.
Super-easy step-by-step cheesemaking

1. Cheese. I. Title.
SF271.T32 1975   637′.3   75-13618
ISBN 0-394-72009-1

Manufactured in the United States of America

INTRODUCTION

Why make your own cheese?
There is something almost magical about the process of trans-
forming milk into firm substantial blocks, wedges and disks
of mellowed-at-home cheese. Home-made cheeses are so
high in quality, so extravagantly taste-tempting with their old-
fashioned country flavor that they would bring delicacy-shop
prices if their equal could be found on your grocer's shelves.
Once you taste curds and whey, ownmade cottage cheese
or home-aged Cheddar, you will realize why more and more
creative gourmet cooks are curdling, pressing and curing their
own cheeses.
The recipes given in this book are home-tested and tasted
and written with step-by-step directions so easy to follow
that mistakes are virtually impossible. If you are the kind
of cook who is intrigued with the unusual, who is always ready
to take on a new challenge . . . cheesemaking is definitely
for you!

HOW TO MAKE THIS BOOK WORK FOR YOU

You may find it helpful to acquaint yourself with the basic cheesemaking procedures before beginning a recipe. These are outlined in the back of the book and are referred to, with page numbers, throughout the text of each recipe.

Contents

THE
CHEESEMAKING
PROCESS
SIMPLIFIED
AND BASIC
INGREDIENTS

CHEESEMAKING SIMPLIFIED

The cheesemaking process consists of the following steps:

1 . . . Curing or ripening the milk by adding buttermilk and heating to 86 degrees F.
2 . . . Curdling the milk by adding rennet and allowing to stand until a firm curd forms
3 . . . Cutting the curd into uniform pieces
4 . . . Cooking the curds by slowly raising the heat until they firm
5 . . . Draining the whey from the curds
6 . . . Salting the curds
7 . . . Hooping and pressing the curds into cheese
8 . . . Drying the cheese and preparing it for storage
9 . . . Curing (aging) the cheese

INGREDIENTS FOR CHEESEMAKING

MILK: The Basic Ingredient. When you make cheese, you ripen, or curdle, milk so that the solid part of it—the curd—separates from the liquid part—the whey.* From this point on, cheeses differ only in the way the curd is cut, cooked, pressed, and cured.

Good cheeses start with good milk. Use only the freshest high-grade pasteurized whole milk or skim milk, or instant nonfat dry milk reconstituted with water.

One gallon of milk will make approximately ¾ pound of hard cheese, 1 pound of soft cheese, or slightly more than a pound of cottage cheese. (The butterfat in milk varies, so you cannot estimate yields exactly.)

If you have your own livestock, making cheese may solve the problem of what to do with surplus milk, but be sure to pasteurize first (*see* Pasteurization, page 52). Goat's milk is

*Save whey for making Ricotta Cheese (*see* page 30) or for baking bread (*see* page 69).

also suitable for making cheese, but be prepared for a subtle difference in flavor.

STARTER: Buttermilk, the natural starter, increases the lactic acid level in milk, helps it to curdle and develops good cheese flavor.

Use only the *freshest* cultured buttermilk with no salt or pre-servatives added. Local dairies in farm communities or health food stores are good sources.

RENNET: When preparing some cheeses, this solidifying enzyme is added to milk to hasten separation of curds and whey and to give the cheesemaker more control over the cur-dling process. Rennet is produced commercially in tablet form and is available at your drugstore or grocery. Ask for junket tablets, which *are* rennet, but don't settle for junket powder, which is not. Rennet is also available by mail (*see* Sources of Supply, page 79).

CHEESE COLOR: An optional ingredient in cheesemaking. It adds nothing to the taste or nutritional value but does give a professional look to your cheese.

Cheese color is available from dairy supply houses (*see* Sources of Supply, page 79).

SALT: An essential for bringing out the flavor of cheese. Coarse, kosher or flake salt works best, but ordinary table salt will do. Coarse salt dissolves slowly and is therefore more easily absorbed, making a tastier finished cheese.

EQUIPMENT

BASIC EQUIPMENT LIST

6 or 8-quart cooking pot of stainless steel or
unchipped enamel
Another larger cooking pot to hold the 8-
quart pot in a double-boiler arrangement
Floating dairy thermometer
Long-handled spoon
Knife with long, stainless-steel blade
Glass measuring cup
Measuring spoons
Cheesecloth
Colander
A deep pan or bowl

DESCRIPTION OF CHEESEMAKING EQUIPMENT

Never buy equipment for cheesemaking unless you absolutely have to. Most cheeses can be made either with equipment you already have around your kitchen or with easily improvised tools.

You'll need the following:

ONE 6 OR 8-QUART COOKING POT: One of stainless steel is best, but any unchipped enamelware or heavily tinned pot will do. Aluminum or galvanized metal is not recommended.

ANOTHER, LARGER CONTAINER: To hold the 6 or 8-quart cooking pot (in a double-boiler arrangement). A large galvanized milk pail, restaurant-sized tin can or water-bath canner will do nicely. This container should ideally be at least 2 inches wider than the cooking pot.

A FLOATING DAIRY THERMOMETER: This is a good investment if you plan to do a lot of cheesemaking, but a candy or jelly thermometer will do if it accurately measures each degree between 75 degrees F. and 175 degrees F.

A SPOON OR STIRRER: Make sure it's long enough to keep your hand well above the liquid level in the cooking pot.

A STAINLESS-STEEL KNIFE: The knife should have a blade long enough to allow you to cut through to the bottom of the pot of cheese without having your hand touch the cheese.

A GLASS MEASURING CUP: With handle.

A SET OF MEASURING SPOONS

CHEESECLOTH

A GOOD-SIZED COLANDER

A DEEP PAN OR BOWL: Large enough to hold the colander.

A CHEESE HOOP: For holding the curds when pressing hard cheeses. Make one from a 2-pound coffee can or 46-ounce juice can. File or sandpaper any jagged or rough edges left around the rim by the can opener. Punch a dozen or more small holes in the bottom of the can from the inside out so the whey can drain during the pressing process.

A FOLLOWER: This is a circular piece of wood or a weight which is set inside the cheese hoop directly over the curds. When pressure is applied, the follower squeezes out the whey and forces the cheese into a solid mass. A store-bought follower is usually made of hardwood, 2 to 4 inches thick, cut ¼-inch smaller than the circumference of the hoop, but you can improvise a follower with a can slightly narrower than the can you use for your hoop. A family-size (13-ounce) tuna-fish can, for example, fits perfectly inside a hoop made from a 2-pound coffee or a 46-ounce tomato-juice can. You may use the can either unopened or empty (with a brick wrapped in aluminum foil set in the empty can). Just be sure that you are able to move the improvised follower up and down with ease.

A CHEESE PRESS: Devise your own from two boards, 1 inch thick and 1 foot square, and a broomstick handle (*see* illustration). Saw the broomstick handle in half to make two dowels. Drill two matching holes at either end of both boards and insert the improvised dowels. The dowels should fit snugly into the bottom board, but the holes in the top board should be large enough for the board to slide easily up and down the dowels. Drill holes, if you like, in the center of the bottom board to allow the whey to drip freely.

In a pinch, you can improvise a press to use with the can-within-a-can method (described on page 7) by simply balancing a board on the inside can (follower) and piling bricks on the board to press the cheese.

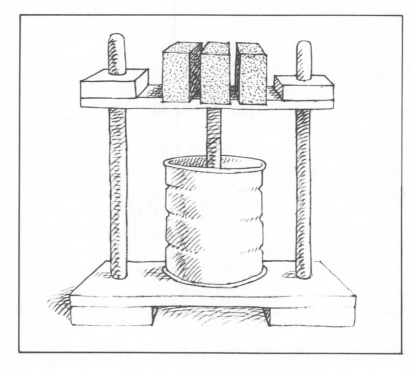

A BANDAGE: For wrapping the cheese when it is pressed. Use several layers of cheesecloth or other light cotton cloth.

ORDINARY CONSTRUCTION BRICKS: You'll need at least eight or ten, or enough rocks or other 4-pound weights to total 30 to 40 pounds. Wrap the bricks, rocks or weights in aluminum foil. Also, you should have a few 1-pound weights.

PARAFFIN: A wax coating to protect the cheese during the aging process.

CURING SHELF: This may be any cool storage place where temperatures range between 50 and 60 degrees F., but never above 70 degrees. A removable shelf is handy because it can be easily scrubbed and sun-dried.

A refrigerator shelf is also fine for storing cheeses, but since temperatures are generally lower than 50 degrees, aging will take a bit longer.

RECIPES

SMALL CURD COTTAGE CHEESE

Homemade cottage cheese is truly a delicacy. There is little resemblance between the bland mass-produced supermarket variety and the utterly delectable fresh-tasting cheese made in your own kitchen.

(Yield: about 1½ pounds)

INGREDIENTS
1 Gallon skim milk
½ Cup instant nonfat dry-milk powder
1 Cup buttermilk   Salt
2 - 3 Tablespoons heavy sweet cream or
sour cream (optional)

EQUIPMENT
All equipment listed in Basic Equipment List
(see page 6).

STEP ONE
CURDLING THE MILK

A. Pour the milk into the smaller cooking pot, add the instant nonfat dry-milk powder and heat to 86 degrees F. (see Curing the Milk, page 54).

B. Stir in the buttermilk.

C. Hold at 86 degrees F. overnight, or for 12 hours, while the milk mixture incubates and forms a curd.

STEP TWO
THE "CLEAN BREAK" TEST

A. Test for curd firmness (*see* "Clean Break" Test II, page 60). In cheeses made without rennet, like this one, the curd may never become tough enough to break smoothly. Proceed with cheesemaking when curd is fairly firm but still a bit custard-like.

STEP THREE
CUTTING THE CURD

A. Cut the curd into ½-inch pieces (*see* Cutting the Curd, page 61).

B. Allow cut curds to stand at 86 degrees F. for 30 minutes while whey separates off.

STEP FOUR
COOKING THE CURD

A. Slowly begin to cook the curds (*see* Cooking the Curds, page 66) until temperature reaches 100 to 104 degrees F. Hold at this temperature for approximately 30 minutes.

STEP FIVE
REMOVING THE WHEY

A. Remove curds from heat as soon as they firm, and remove whey (*see* Removing the Whey, page 68).

STEP SIX
SALTING THE CURDS

A. Season cheese to your liking with coarse salt (*see* Salting the Curds, page 70).

B. Refrigerate cheese.

STEP SEVEN
ADDING CREAM

A. If you like a creamier cheese, stir a few tablespoons of heavy sweet cream or sour cream into your cooled cheese.

B. Keep cheese well refrigerated.

LARGE CURD COTTAGE CHEESE

Large curd cottage cheese is prepared in essentially the same way as the small curd variety, differing only in the addition of rennet, which curdles the milk mixture in less time. The result is a milder and less acid cottage cheese with a distinct mellow flavor.

(Yield: about 1½ pounds)

INGREDIENTS
1 Gallon skim milk
½ Cup instant nonfat dry-milk powder
1 Cup buttermilk
¼ Rennet tablet
2 - 3 Tablespoons heavy sweet cream or
sour cream (optional)

EQUIPMENT
All equipment mentioned in Basic
Equipment List (see page 6).

STEP ONE
CURDLING THE MILK

A. Mix skim milk and dry milk and bring them to 86 degrees F. (see Heating the Milk, page 54).

B. Stir in buttermilk.

C. Dissolve ¼ rennet tablet in 2 tablespoons cold water and add to milk mixture. Stir in thoroughly.

D. Leave milk mixture undisturbed in its warm water bath for 3 to 5 hours.

STEP TWO
THE "CLEAN BREAK" TEST

A. Test curd for proper firmness. Follow the directions given for The "Clean Break" Test, page 58.

STEP THREE
CUTTING THE CURD

A. When curd tests firm, cut into ½-inch pieces according to directions given on page 61 (Cutting the Curd).

B. Replace pot of cut curds in the water bath and keep at 86 degrees F. for 30 minutes to firm curds slightly. Turn the heat on and off under the water bath as necessary to keep the curd temperature constant.

STEP FOUR
COOKING THE CURD

A. Slowly raise temperature of curds to between 100 and 104 degrees F. Follow precisely directions given in Cooking the Curds, page 66.

B. Hold curds at this temperature for 30 to 60 minutes. If curds still crumble when a few are squeezed gently in your hand, gradually raise the heat to between 110 and 115 degrees F. as described in Cooking the Curds. Do not overcook!

C. When the curds are just firm enough, remove them from the heat and skim off the whey (*see* Removing the Whey, page 68).

STEP FIVE
SALTING THE CURDS

A. After the curds have been drained, add salt (*see* Salting the Curds, page 70).

B. Refrigerate the cheese.

STEP SIX
ADDING CREAM

A. Cottage cheese is greatly improved if a few tablespoons of sweet or sour cream are stirred in after cheese has been chilled.

B. Store cheese in refrigerator until used.

POT CHEESE

Pot cheese, like cottage cheese, is always made from skim milk. It is unique in that its curds are somewhat less zesty than those of cottage cheese because of the addition of rennet just before acid coagulation. The homemade variety is really delectable.

(Yield: about 2 pounds)

INGREDIENTS
1 Gallon skim milk
½ Cup instant nonfat dry-milk powder
1 Cup buttermilk
⅛ Rennet tablet
Salt

EQUIPMENT
All equipment listed in Basic Equipment List
(see page 6).

STEP ONE
CURDLING THE MILK

A. Bring milk to room temperature, stir in instant nonfat dry-milk powder and starter, and warm mixture over hot water until your thermometer reads 86 degrees F. (see Curing the Milk, page 54).

B. Cover the cooking pot and allow the milk to stand undisturbed at this temperature for 5 hours.

C. Dissolve rennet thoroughly in ¼ cup cold water, and stir into milk mixture only long enough for even distribution.

STEP TWO
THE "CLEAN BREAK" TEST

With temperature still at 86 degrees F., begin testing the curd for firmness about 1 to 1¼ hours after adding rennet (*see* "Clean Break" Test, page 58).

STEP THREE
CUTTING THE CURD

A. As soon as curd breaks away cleanly, cut it into pieces approximately ⅜-inch square (*see* Cutting the Curd, page 61).

B. Allow cut curds to stand at 86 degrees F. for 30 minutes.

STEP FOUR
COOKING THE CURD

A. Gradually raise heat in the outer container until the curd temperature reaches 104 degrees F. (*see* Cooking the Curd, page 66). Stir the curds very gently with spoon or hand to permit even distribution of heat as temperature increases.

B. Hold curds at 104 degrees F. for 30 to 60 minutes, stirring occasionally to keep them from sticking together.

C. Test curds by squeezing a few gently in your hand. If they are still too soft, increase curd temperature *very gradually* to between 115 and 120 degrees F. Stir curds frequently and test for firmness every 10 minutes.

STEP FIVE
REMOVING THE WHEY

A. As soon as curds are firm enough, remove cooking pot from heat and pour curds and whey into a cheesecloth-lined colander set over a deep bowl.

B. Drain for a minute or two, then dip cheesecloth filled with curds into lukewarm water to rinse. Drain again, then turn the curds into a large bowl.

STEP SIX
SALTING THE CURDS

A. Add salt to taste and mix to distribute evenly (*see* Salting the Curds, page 70).

B. Pack cheese into containers, cover tightly and refrigerate before using.

FARMER CHEESE

Farmer cheese differs from cottage cheese only in that it is made from whole rather than skimmed milk and that it is lightly pressed into a rectangular shape. The fresh, mellow flavor needs no dressing or herbs to enhance it.

(Yield: about 1¼ pounds)

INGREDIENTS

1 Gallon whole milk
½ Cup instant nonfat dry-milk powder
1½ Cups buttermilk
2 Tablespoons heavy cream (if served unpressed)

EQUIPMENT

All equipment listed in Basic Equipment List, page 6, plus one 1-pound weight.

STEP ONE
CURDLING THE MILK

A. Combine milk, instant nonfat dry milk and starter in smaller pot, and stir until thoroughly mixed.

B. Heat mixture to 86 degrees F. (*see* Heating the Milk, page 54). This should take 1 hour. If, at the end of this time, the temperature is lower than 86 degrees F., turn heat on under larger pot for a few seconds. It is important that the temperature of the milk mixture not rise above 88 degrees F. during this stage of cheesemaking.

C. Hold temperature at 86 degrees F. overnight, or 12 hours, by leaving the mixture covered in the pan of warm water over the pilot light of your kitchen stove, or if your stove has no pilot light, wrap the large pan in a blanket. By morning the curd will be formed.

Note: Remember that the curd will not be quite as firm as in cheeses made with rennet. Cut the curd anyway and proceed as directed.

STEP TWO
CUTTING THE CURD

A. Cut the curd in pieces about ⅜-inch thick (*see* Cutting the Curd, page 61).

B. Allow cut curds to stand for 30 minutes at 86 degrees F. while whey separates off.

STEP THREE
COOKING THE CURDS

A. Gradually raise heat to 104 degrees F., stirring gently from time to time with your hand (*see* Cooking the Curds, page 66). It is important that temperatures be precise.

B. Cook the cut curds slowly at 104 degrees F. for 30 to 40 minutes. Be careful not to break up curds as you stir. Test curds from time to time while cooking by squeezing a handful very, very gently. If curds hold some shape, they are ready. Do not overcook! Remember, this is an unaged cheese, so you cannot count on extra months of aging to soften it and compensate for errors in cooking.

STEP FOUR
REMOVING THE WHEY

A. As soon as curds are fairly firm, dip off whey (*see* Removing the Whey, page 68). If the rinsing seems to be breaking the curds, stop immediately. Cheese that is to be eaten within 2 or 3 days needs very little rinsing.

STEP FIVE
SALTING THE CURDS

Chill curds for 20 minutes before adding salt to taste.

STEP SIX
PRESSING THE CHEESE

Farmer cheese is traditionally lightly pressed into a rectangular shape.

A. Spread a long piece of cheesecloth (or similar cotton cloth) on a flat surface. Fold it into a long narrow strip the width you want your cheese to be. Allow for a bit of overlap on the top and sides.

B. Pile cheese in center of cheesecloth and shape into a rectangle. Fold ends of bandage over curds, place in a plastic freezer container (or other rectangular mold) and cover with aluminum foil. Press with a 1-pound weight until moisture is drawn out into the bandage and cheese holds its shape.

C. Unwrap bandage and refrigerate cheese in waxed paper or plastic wrap until ready to use.

D. Farmer cheese may be served unpressed. In this case, after it is salted and chilled, stir in 2 tablespoons heavy cream and pack the cheese in an attractive glass mold. (A freezer container will do.) Chill the cheese until serving time, unmold, sprinkle with salt and freshly ground pepper and serve with crackers or fresh vegetables.

RENNETED FARMER CHEESE

If you prefer farmer cheese that has a rather dry, stiff consistency, use rennet for a firmer curd.

A. Dissolve ⅛ rennet tablet in ¼ cup of cool water. Stir in rennet as soon as milk mixture reaches 86 degrees F., and mix thoroughly.

B. Cut the coagulated curd into ¼-inch pieces (see Cutting the Curd, page 61). Allow cut curds to stand at 86 degrees F. for 30 minutes.

C. Proceed to cook, drain and salt as directed for unrenneted farmer cheese.

D. Farmer cheese prepared with rennet needs a little heavier pressing than the bandage method described above. To press, line your hoop with cheesecloth and spoon in the curds. Cut a cheesecloth circle to fit and lay it on top. Insert a follower over the top of the circle and set the hoop in the press (see Hooping and Pressing, page 71). Apply pressure *very* lightly to begin, increasing it gradually as you go along, but press only with 10 pounds of weight.

E. Remove cheese from hoop, unwrap and refrigerate in plastic bag as soon as the moisture content is reduced and the cheese is firm enough for your taste. Store in refrigerator.

CREAM CHEESE

This smooth, creamy, delicately flavored cheese is generally used fresh as a spread. It is easy to make and unusually tasty either served plain or combined with herbs.

(Yield: about ½ pound)

INGREDIENTS
4 Cups sour cream
½ Rennet tablet
½ Teaspoon salt

EQUIPMENT
1 Glass or stainless-steel double boiler
Dairy thermometer
Cheesecloth or similar cotton cloth

STEP ONE
CURDLING THE CREAM

A. Measure sour cream into 1-quart saucepan.

B. Crush ½ rennet tablet and mix with 2 tablespoons water. Dissolve completely.

C. Stir the rennet solution into the cream. Mix thoroughly.

STEP TWO
COOKING THE CREAM

A. Place saucepan with sour cream mixture over hot water and bring the temperature of the mixture very slowly to 100 degrees F.

B. Hold the sour-cream mixture at this temperature for 20 minutes by turning the heat off and on under the double boiler as necessary.

STEP THREE
COOLING THE CREAM

A. Remove top of the double boiler holding the curdled cream, and set aside to cool to room temperature.

B. Spoon cream into a double-thick cheesecloth square. Tie corners of cheesecloth together to form a bag.

C. Hang the bag in a cool place free from drafts, with a bowl set underneath to catch whey. (Your kitchen faucet spout is an ideal spot.)

D. Untie bag every few hours to check firmness of cheese.

STEP FOUR
SALTING THE CHEESE

A. When cheese is completely drained and quite firm, remove from the cheesecloth and place in a bowl.

B. Mix in salt, form the cheese into a bar and wrap in wax paper or aluminum foil. Refrigerate.

FRESH HERB CHEESE

This herb cheese—like Boursin—has an unsurpassed quality and taste. Homemade cottage cheese adds a freshness that is difficult to duplicate, but even the grocery-store variety is delicious prepared this way.

(Yield: about 1 pound)

INGREDIENTS
4 Cloves garlic, peeled
1 Teaspoon salt
¼ Cup fresh herbs, minced (Almost any combination will do, but rosemary, chives, parsley, sage and/or thyme are best. Two tablespoons dried herbs may be substituted for the fresh ones, but the flavor will not be as subtle.)
8 Ounces homemade cream cheese
½ Cup sour cream
¼ Cup heavy cream
8 Ounces fresh homemade cottage cheese

A. Crush garlic with salt, using a mortar and pestle. Add minced herbs and crush again.

B. Beat cream cheese until fluffy and continue beating while you add sour cream, heavy cream and cottage cheese. Add the garlic and herbs and beat until well blended.

C. Spoon cheese onto large double-thick square of cheesecloth and tie opposite ends together to form a bag. Knot ends of cheesecloth around the handle of a wooden spoon and suspend cheese over a deep bowl or large cracker tin.

D. Allow moisture to drip from cheese for at least 24 hours. Refrigerate cheese if there are flies about, or if it is very hot. Occasionally retie the bag to make it tighter as the cheese loses moisture and compacts slightly.

E. To serve, untie cheesecloth and turn cheese, seam-side down, on a plate. Chill.

RICOTTA CHEESE

Ricotta, a fresh, moist cheese with a sweet, nutlike flavor, has soft curds similar in texture to cottage cheese. Since Ricotta can be made from any fresh whey left over from a cheese made with rennet, you can save time and money by preparing this and a hard cheese (perhaps Parmesan-Style Italian Grating Cheese, *see* page 43) on the same day.

(Yield: just under 1 pound)

INGREDIENTS
1 Gallon whey
6 Cups whole milk
½ Cup strong vinegar
Salt

EQUIPMENT
Large container
Long-handled spoon
Cheesecloth
Hoop

STEP ONE
CURING THE MILK

A. If you are making Ricotta along with Italian grating cheese, simply heat whey as soon as the curd chunk goes into the hoop. (Otherwise, collect and freeze enough whey from other cheesemaking sessions.)

B. Heat whey until a layer of cream rises to the surface, stir in whole milk, then continue to heat until *just under* the boiling point. *Do not boil!*

STEP TWO
CURDLING THE MILK

A. Allow to stand off the heat until curd forms. As soon as curd rises and pulls away from sides of pan, stir in vinegar thoroughly.

B. Skim off curds as soon as they rise once more and heap them into a cloth-lined hoop.

C. Set the cheese aside to drain for about 8 hours.

D. Salt to taste after draining (*see* Salting the Curd, page 70). Chill before serving.
Note: If you are continuing with the recipe for Italian grating cheese, place cheese and hoop back in the hot whey as soon as the Ricotta curds have been set in their hoop.

MOZZARELLA CHEESE

This delicate Italian cheese with its fragile flavor and interesting texture needs no curing. Make it today and eat it tomorrow.
(Yield: 1 pound)

INGREDIENTS
5 Quarts whole milk
1 Cup buttermilk
½ Rennet tablet   Salt

EQUIPMENT
All equipment listed in Basic Equipment List,
page 6.
Hoop and Press

STEP ONE
CURDLING THE MILK

A. Bring milk to 86 degrees F. (*see* Heating the Milk, page 54).

B. Stir in buttermilk.

C. Dissolve rennet in 2 tablespoons cool water and add to milk mixture (*see* Curdling the Milk, Method II, page 55). It should take about 45 minutes for the curd to form.

STEP TWO
THE "CLEAN BREAK" TEST

Test curd for proper firmness (*see* The "Clean Break" Test, page 58).

STEP THREE
BREAKING UP THE CURD

A. In making mozzarella cheese the curd is broken, not cut. Heat curd as hot as your hand can stand, then use your hand to break curd into small pieces.

B. Stir and break up any large pieces until the curds begin to firm and squeak when you chew on a few.

C. Remove curds from heat, and skim off the whey (*see* Removing the Whey, page 68). Do not discard the whey. You'll need it later.

STEP FOUR
SALTING THE CURDS

Drain the curds and add salt (*see* Salting the Curds, page 70).

STEP FIVE
HOOPING AND PRESSING THE CHEESE

A. Follow directions given in Hooping and Pressing the Cheese, page 71. Use a total of 20 pounds' pressure.

B. Heat the whey over low heat to 180 degrees F.

C. Remove cheese from hoop, unwrap and place in heated whey, off the heat.

D. Cover the pot and let stand until cool.

E. Remove cooled cheese from whey and let drain for 24 hours. Eat the cheese as is or use it in other recipes.

MUENSTER CHEESE

Muenster, a mellow, buttery-soft cheese, has a springy texture and a creamy-white interior. Usually made from whole milk and sometimes flavored with caraway seeds, Muenster is absolutely delicious when eaten fresh; however, if you prefer a slightly sour flavor, the cheese can be aged for a few months.

(Yield: about 1 pound)

INGREDIENTS

1 Gallon whole milk
¼ Cup instant nonfat dry-milk powder
1 Cup buttermilk
1 Rennet tablet
Salt to taste
Caraway seeds to taste (optional)

EQUIPMENT

All equipment listed in Basic Equipment List
(see page 6)
Hoop and Press

STEP ONE
CURING THE MILK

A. Measure milk into 8-quart pot. Stir in dry milk and starter.

B. Slowly bring the mixture to 86 degrees F. over hot water and hold at that temperature for 3 hours (see Curdling the Milk, page 55).

STEP TWO
CURDLING THE MILK

A. Crush rennet and dissolve thoroughly in ¼ cup cool water. Add to milk mixture and stir for 1 minute.

B. Let stand undisturbed at 86 degrees F. until the curd tests firm (see The "Clean Break" Test, page 58).

STEP THREE
CUTTING THE CURD

Cut the firm curd into ¾-inch pieces by slicing across vertically and diagonally in both directions (see Cutting the Curd, page 61).

STEP FOUR
COOKING THE CURDS

A. Increase curd temperature to 90 degrees F. (see Cooking the Curd, page 66). Maintain this temperature for 2 hours while the curds soak, then raise the heat gradually to 104 degrees F. Test for firmness by cooling and squeezing a handful of curds. If the curds still seem soft after 1 hour's cooking, begin to increase the heat gradually until the curds firm slightly.

STEP FIVE
REMOVING THE WHEY

A. Remove curds from heat and skim off as much whey as possible.

B. Pour curds into cheesecloth-lined colander set over a deep bowl (see Removing the Whey, page 68).

STEP SIX
SALTING THE CURDS

A. After curds have cooled a bit, rinse carefully by dipping them (cheesecloth and all) in lukewarm water (*see* Rinsing the Curds, page 69).

B. Drain for 10 minutes and add salt and caraway seeds to taste (*see* Salting the Curds, page 70).

STEP SEVEN
HOOPING AND PRESSING THE CHEESE

A. Spoon curds into cloth-lined hoop while still fairly warm, cover with cheesecloth circle and place follower on top (*see* Hooping and Pressing the Cheese, page 71).

B. Set hoop in press and add weights one at a time to reach a pressure of 10 to 15 pounds. The cheese may be eaten ripe or aged in the refrigerator for several months.

CHEDDAR CHEESE

The best Cheddar I have *ever* tasted is a cheese I made last year using this recipe.

(Yield: about 1 to 1¼ pounds)

INGREDIENTS

1 Gallon whole milk
1 Cup buttermilk
Cheese color (optional)
1 Rennet tablet
1 Tablespoon salt

EQUIPMENT

All equipment listed in Basic Equipment List
(*see* page 6)
Wire roasting rack
Roasting pan
Hoop and Press

STEP ONE
CURING THE MILK

Measure milk into 8-quart pot. Stir in starter. Cover pot and allow mixture to stand for at least 4 hours (or overnight) at room temperature (72 degrees F.).

STEP TWO
CURDLING THE MILK

A. Slowly bring milk mixture to 86 degrees F. over hot water (*see* Curdling the Milk, Method II, page 55). Add cheese color, if desired (*see* Adding Color, page 57).

B. Slowly raise milk temperature to 88-90 degrees F.; add rennet mixed in ¼ cup cool water as instructed in Curdling the Milk, Method II, page 55. Remove from heat. Cover and let stand until curd tests firm (see The "Clean Break" Test, page 58). This should take from 30 to 40 minutes.

STEP THREE
CUTTING THE CURD

A. Cut the firm curd into ½-inch pieces by slicing across vertically and diagonally in both directions with long-bladed knife (see Cutting the Curd, page 61).

B. Use your hand to gently stir the curds for 15 minutes, with long, slow, sweeping movements. Rough or rapid stirring will break up the curds. Cut any large curds into ½-inch pieces.

STEP FOUR
COOKING THE CURDS

A. Increase curd temperature gradually to 100 degrees F. (see Cooking the Curds, page 66). Stir gently every 3 to 5 minutes.

B. Hold curds at 100-102 degrees F., stirring every few minutes, until they test firm. This should take between 30 and 60 minutes.

C. Remove from heat and allow curds to stand in whey for 1 hour, or until they toughen somewhat. Stir every 5 to 10 minutes.

STEP FIVE
REMOVING THE WHEY

A. Scoop off as much whey as possible. Pour curds into a cheesecloth-lined colander (*see* Removing the Whey, page 68).

B. Hold two ends of cheesecloth in each hand. Using a rolling motion, tilt curds back and forth to drain off excess whey.

STEP SIX
OVEN-COOKING THE CURDS

A. Turn oven temperature to warm. Drape a double layer of cheesecloth over a wire roasting rack. Set rack in a roasting pan. Carefully heap curds onto the cheesecloth in a layer 1 inch thick.

B. Check oven temperature with your thermometer. The curds must cook at *exactly* 98 degrees F. Correct temperature is *very* important. Keep thermometer in oven next to pan of curds. If necessary, turn oven on and off to maintain even temperature.

C. Cook curds until they mat together in a large mass (about 20 minutes). Slice the curd mass into 1-inch strips.

D. Continue to cook sliced strips, maintaining heat at 98 degrees F., for 1 hour. Turn each strip *every* 15 minutes to allow *even* cooking.

STEP SEVEN
SALTING THE CURDS

A. Remove curd strips from oven and cut into approximately 1-inch squares.

B. Set cheese squares in colander and salt as directed in Salting the Curds, page 70. Allow salted curds to stand for 20 minutes.

STEP EIGHT
HOOPING AND PRESSING THE CHEESE

A. Spoon curds into cloth-lined hoop, cover with cheesecloth circle and place follower on top (*see* Hooping and Pressing the Cheese, page 71).

B. Set hoop in press. Add weights one at a time to reach a total of 12 to 16 pounds. Press for 5 to 10 minutes. Remove weights and follower, and pour off whey.

C. Replace follower and return hoop to press. Add weights one at a time to reach a total of 25 to 30 pounds. Maintain this pressure for 30 to 60 minutes or until cheese is very firm.

D. Turn cheese out of its hoop and unwrap cloth liner.

Smooth out the cheese surface (*see* Drying the Cheese, page 74). Bandage the cheese as directed (*see* Hooping and Pressing the Cheese, page 71), and return cheese to hoop. Replace follower.

E. Add weights one at a time until the total reaches 24 to 30 pounds. Press for 16 to 20 hours.

STEP NINE
DRYING, SEALING AND AGING

A. Unwrap cheese from its bandage. Wipe the cheese surface and check for imperfections. Dip in warm water and smooth with your fingers if necessary.

B. Dry (*see* Drying the Cheese, page 74) and seal with paraffin if desired (*see* Sealing the Cheese for Aging, page 75). Age the cheese (*see* Aging the Cheese, page 77) for 6 to 8 weeks for mild Cheddar flavor. Age for 3 to 5 months if you like a sharp cheese, and longer if you prefer extra sharp flavor.

PARMESAN-STYLE ITALIAN GRATING CHEESE

Made with whole milk and rennet, this cheese can be eaten fresh when it is soft, or used when it has been salted, soaked in brine and then cured for several months to produce a hard cheese marvelous for grating. Save the whey after cooking the curds—you can use it to make Ricotta Cheese (*see* page 30).

(Yield: about 1 pound)

INGREDIENTS
5 Quarts whole milk
½ Rennet tablet
Salt

EQUIPMENT
All equipment listed in Basic Equipment List,
page 6
Hoop and Press

STEP ONE
CURDLING THE MILK

A. Measure milk into 8-quart container. Heat to 86 degrees F. (*see* Curdling the Milk, page 55).

B. Dissolve rennet in 2 tablespoons cool water and mix thoroughly into warm milk. Cover the pot and maintain the 86 degree F. temperature until the curd tests firm (*see* The "Clean Break" Test, page 58). The curd should set in about 40 minutes.

STEP TWO
CUTTING THE CURD

A. Cut curd into ¾-inch pieces with long-bladed knife (*see* Cutting the Curd, page 61).

B. Heat curds and whey until they are as hot as your hands can stand, then press hot curds together into one solid lump. Keep the whey remaining in the pot. You will need it again later.

STEP THREE
HOOPING AND PRESSING THE CURDS

A. Lift curd mass from whey and set into cheese hoop (*see* Hooping and Pressing the Curds, page 71).

B. Insert follower over curds and press until cheese takes on a fairly firm shape (about 10 pounds' weight should be enough).

C. Pull cheese and wrapping out of hoop, turn cheese upside down and set back into hoop. Press cheese again only long enough to firm it well.

STEP FOUR
COOKING THE CHEESE

A. Set cheese, hoop and all, back in whey, and heat until the whey is *just below* the boiling point. *Do not boil!*

B. Remove pot from heat and allow hooped cheese to cool to room temperature in whey.

C. Remove cheese in the hoop from the whey and drain in hoop for 24 hours.

D. Remove cheese from hoop and serve fresh, or age further and use for grating.

STEP FIVE
AGING THE CHEESE

This cheese is bland and not very interesting when fresh but when aged and used as a grating cheese it is really delicious. Although the recipe calls for 4 to 6 months of aging, the cheese will be quite hard and ready to use after about 2 months. The flavor becomes sharper the longer it ages.

A. To make a hard grating cheese, rub the new cheese well with 2 tablespoons table salt after removing from the hoop. Set on a cool storage shelf (50 to 55 degrees F.) or in the refrigerator and let dry for 3 or 4 days.

B. When surface is quite dry, prepare a strong brine of 2 pounds of salt dissolved in 2 quarts of water.

C. Leave cheese in this brine for 4 days, then take it out, wipe dry and rub surface thoroughly with salt once again.

D. Set aside to dry in a cool storage spot for 4 to 6 months. Rub lightly with salt once a week for the first 3 or 4 weeks, turning each time it is salted to dry evenly on all sides. Repeat salting and turning from then on at intervals of 2 to 3 weeks. Should any mold form on the rind, rub the spot with salt until it disappears.

THE PROCESS
DESCRIBED

CLEANLINESS IN CHEESEMAKING

Because milk and milk products present an almost irresistible attraction to bacteria, take special precautions to keep your equipment spotless. Scrub all utensils with soap and hot water immediately after using and rinse thoroughly with boiling water. Wash cheesecloth (or other cloths) with soap and water immediately after using, boil them, and if possible, hang in the sun to dry.

Scrub the curing cupboard or shelf (see page 9) with soap and water at least once a week while the cheese is aging. If conditions permit, dry curing shelf in the sun.

Dairymen often use a chlorine solution on their equipment to prevent contamination. If you like, obtain some for your own use from a drug or hardware store. Follow the manufacturer's directions *precisely* and *rinse very carefully afterwards with several changes of water.*

Desirable and somewhat exotic strains of mold may be imported from other countries and introduced into cheesemaking to produce such delectable gourmet cheeses as Roquefort, Stilton or Brie. However, most molds that attack homemade cheeses arrive totally uninvited. To guard against these, make sure there are no cracks or holes in your cheese before setting to dry (see Drying Your Cheese, page 74). Dip into hot paraffin only when cheese is perfectly dry.

When mold does appear, as it sometimes will, scrape it off immediately! As long as the mold is confined to the surface, the cheese will still be edible. If mold extends clear through the cheese, throw it away.

PASTEURIZATION

The authorities in most countries are of the opinion that the aging process eliminates any harmful organisms in milk, but it is against the law in the United States to make cheese for sale with any but pasteurized milk. You may use whole, skim, partially skimmed or powdered milk for your cheesemaking, and unless you raise your own cows, the milk you use will almost certainly be pasteurized.

Reconstituted instant whole or skim milk used in cheesemaking must also be pasteurized, since the water you add may contain troublemaking bacteria. Pasteurization kills these, along with any other organisms which may be unhealthy or which give off-flavors to your cheese.

A. Heat water in the larger container, pour milk into the 8-quart container and set this in the hot water to improvise a double boiler. While water in the larger pot heats, stir milk constantly to keep it from scorching or sticking. When milk temperature reaches 145 degrees F., turn off heat and maintain temperature for 30 minutes. (This may require that the heat be turned on and off, so keep an eye on the thermometer and your hand on the stove knob.)

B. Cool milk quickly to 86 degrees F. by immersing the 8-quart pot in cold water. If you are interrupted and cheesemaking must be put off, bring milk to 50 degrees F. and refrigerate until you are ready to begin again.

FLASH METHOD

A. You can also pasteurize milk by heating to 161 degrees F. (following the method described above) and holding the milk at this high temperature for only 30 seconds. The trouble with this method is that you run the risk of scorching, or worse, boiling the milk. If you opt for "flash pasteurization," control the temperature carefully.

B. Always lower temperature quickly by immersing the pot of milk in cold water. Stir occasionally to ensure even cooling. Should a crisis arise and cheesemaking be put off, bring milk quickly to 50 degrees F. and refrigerate until you are ready to begin again.

CURING THE MILK

STEP ONE
HEATING THE MILK

A. Fill you larger container ⅓ full of warm water (not hotter than 92 degrees F.) and set it on the stove. Do not turn on heat.

B. Place the cooking pot of milk into the large container in a double-boiler arrangement. Allow to stand for 1 hour.

STEP TWO
TAKING THE TEMPERATURE OF THE MILK

A. Measure the temperature of the milk with your dairy thermometer. If it registers less than 86 degrees F., turn the heat on under the large container for 2 to 3 minutes. Wait 15 minutes, then measure the temperature of the milk once more. Continue this process until the milk warms to 86 degrees F. Occasionally the milk will accidentally be warmed to a temperature higher than 86 degrees. In this case, wait until the milk cools before adding the starter.

CURDLING THE MILK

Curdling is the point at which the curd, or solid part of the milk, thickens and separates from the whey, or liquid part.
Milk is curdled in one of two ways:

FIRST METHOD
CURDLING THE MILK USING A BUTTERMILK STARTER

The cheesemaker brings the milk to 86 degrees F. and adds buttermilk (a lactic acid-producing starter). The mixture is held at this temperature until acid develops and causes a curd to form, usually within 12 hours.

SECOND METHOD
CURDLING THE MILK USING A BUTTERMILK AND RENNET STARTER

The cheesemaker brings the milk to 86 degrees F. and adds a buttermilk starter. Acid production begins. The cheesemaker then adds rennet, which speeds the curdling process.

STEP ONE
ADDING THE STARTER

A. Add the buttermilk starter, stir it in thoroughly, then cover to retain the heat. Place the container and cooking pot over the pilot light of your stove or in your oven to maintain the correct temperature throughout the curdling process. Allow the milk to stand *undisturbed* until it curdles.

STEP TWO
ADDING THE RENNET

A. If (and *only* if) your recipe calls for rennet, break the tablet and crush the portion called for in your recipe in a little boiled and cooled water. Stir it in at the specified time to shorten the curdling process and to firm the curd.

ADDING COLOR

Natural cheeses range in color from creamy white to pale yellow depending on the season and the diet of the cow. If you prefer more commercial-looking cheeses, add color to suit your taste.

A. Color is available in tablet, cake or liquid form (*see* Sources of Supply, page 79). Always follow specific directions provided by manufacturer.

B. Add color with a light hand unless you prefer a bright-orange tint.

C. If tablet is used, always crush and dissolve completely in cool water before adding to cheese, or finished cheese may have a rash of orange freckles.

D. Stir in color thoroughly as soon as milk reaches incubation temperature.

E. Always add color *before* adding rennet.

THE "CLEAN BREAK" TEST

This test is most effective for cheeses made with rennet. In some cheeses made without this firming agent the curd may never become tough enough to break smoothly. Proceed with cheesemaking anyway if the curd is fairly firm but still a bit custard-like.

TEST I

A. Insert one finger at an angle into center of the curd.

B. Bring your thumb down to meet your finger.

C. Lift your finger up. If the curd breaks cleanly over your finger and clear whey fills the depression, the curd is ready to cut.

TEST II

A. Flatten your knife against the inside of the cooking pot.

B. Press the curd toward the center. The curd is ready to be cut when it breaks away quickly and smoothly from the sides of the pot.

CUTTING THE CURD

You'll know the curd has formed when the top is firm-looking and a small amount of clear liquid (whey) appears on the surface. Use one of the "Clean Break" tests to determine when the curd is firm enough to cut (see illustration, page 59).

STEP ONE
MAKING THE FIRST CUTS

The general rule is to cut two ways vertically and then two ways diagonally (see illustration, page 62).

A. Begin by inserting your knife to the bottom of the pot on the side of the cooking pot directly opposite you.

B. Pull the knife toward you in a clean vertical stroke. Remove the knife carefully and continue to cut parallel lines at the intervals specified in your recipe.

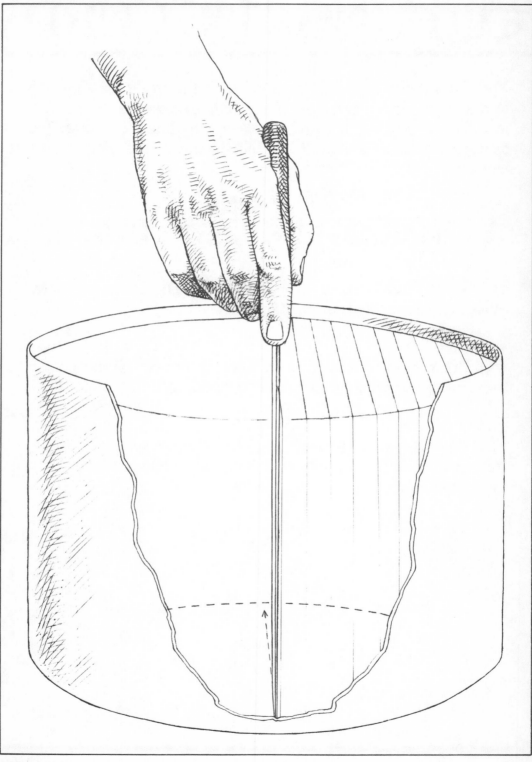

STEP TWO
MAKING THE SECOND CUTS

A. Turn cooking pot a quarter of the way around. Repeat the series of parallel cuts, drawing knife toward you in lines exactly perpendicular to previous cuts.

B. Turn cooking pot back to original position; then, holding knife at a slant, start at one side and cut through curd at an angle, using deep diagonal strokes. Follow original cuts as closely as possible.

C. Turn cooking pot once more and make diagonal cuts in the opposite direction. Don't worry if all of the curd cubes are not uniform. Cut the larger ones down to size while they cook.

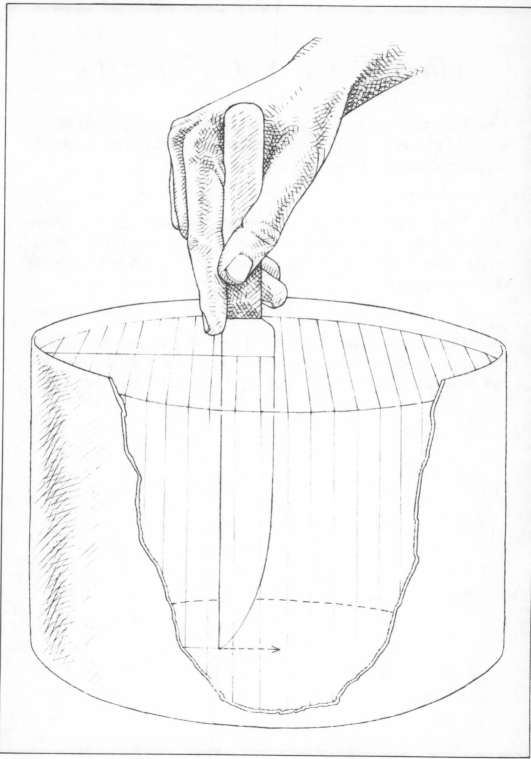

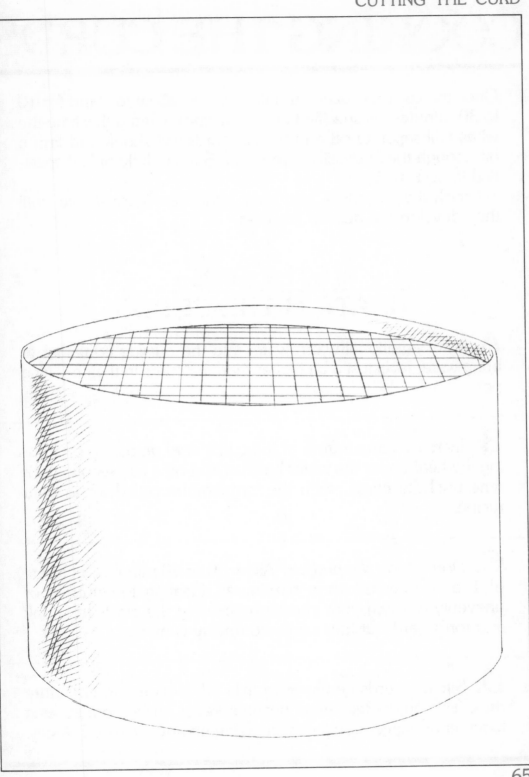

COOKING THE CURDS

Once the curd has been cut into squares, allow to stand for 10 to 30 minutes (as specified in your recipe). During this time the whey will separate off and the cut curds will shrink and firm a bit, though they will still be very soft. Stir carefully only if specified in your recipe.

To cook the cut curds, you must heat them *very slowly* until they develop the desired firmness.

STEP ONE
HEATING THE CURDS

A. Pour additional warm water into the *outside* container to bring water level just a bit higher than the curds in their cooking pot.

B. Increase temperature of the curds *very gradually* by turning the heat under the water bath on and off a few seconds at a time until the curds reach the temperature called for in your recipe.

C. *Don't hurry the process.* Allow 30 or 40 minutes, or a rate of 1 or 2 degrees every 5 minutes. Heating too quickly or unevenly will ruin your cheese by causing the curds to shrink and form hard outsides and soft, mushy centers.

D. Stir the curds gently once in a while as the temperature rises. This guarantees even heating, keeps curds from sticking together and gives you a chance to cut up any oversized pieces.

E. The curds will firm and separate from the whey as they heat. They require more frequent gentle stirring at this point.

STEP TWO
HOLDING THE HEAT

A. To hold curds at temperature called for in your recipe, turn heat on and off under the large pot of water a few seconds at a time.

B. Let curds stand at this temperature the length of time directed in your recipe. Stir occasionally to keep them from massing and melting together.

STEP THREE
TESTING THE CURDS FOR FIRMNESS

A. When properly firm, curds should have the consistency of well-formed scrambled eggs, with pieces that are individual but not rubbery.

B. If curds refuse to firm, increase temperature gradually to 10 degrees higher than your recipe calls for. In this case, stir more frequently. Take care not to scald the curds. Overheating means death to good cheese, while undercooked curds can usually be salvaged.

REMOVING THE WHEY

Cooking the curds properly is the trickiest step in cheesemaking. To avoid undercooking or overcooking, ask yourself these questions:

- Did you allow the curds to stand for 10 to 30 minutes after cutting them?
- Did you bring the heat up *very* slowly?
- Did you have the patience to allow temperature to rise those last few degrees with the heat turned off to prevent too rapid a rise?
- Did you remember to stir the curds and move those in the center toward the outside rim so that all would be heated evenly?

When the curds are firm, it is time to separate them from the whey.

STEP ONE
PREPARING THE COLANDER

A. Cut a piece of cheesecloth 24" × 48", fold in half and drape over colander in a double-thick layer.

B. Set the cheesecloth-lined colander over a deep bowl.

STEP TWO
SCOOPING OFF THE WHEY

A. Use glass measuring cup to dip off as much whey as possible without crushing the curds. (Freeze the whey in 1-cup containers and substitute for water or milk when baking bread.)

STEP THREE
POURING OFF THE WHEY

A. Pour curds and remaining whey into cloth-lined colander.

B. Hold two corners of the cheesecloth in each hand, fold cloth over so curds cannot fall out, and tip curds back and forth for several minutes to drain off whey.

STEP FOUR
RINSING THE CURDS

A. Rinse curds by dipping them (in the folded cloth) into bowl of lukewarm water.

B. Tie opposite corners of cheesecloth together to form a bag. Hang bag of curds over sink spigot or suspend over empty bowl by slipping a wooden spoon through the knot. Allow to drip for 30 minutes.

STEP FIVE
COOLING THE CURDS

A. Untie cheesecloth bag and empty curds into a large bowl. Stir gently with a spoon or your hand every few minutes to prevent curds from matting together.

SALTING THE CURDS

Flavor your cheese with either ordinary fine (table) or coarse (flake or kosher) salt. Coarse salt is generally preferred, since it dissolves more slowly and is therefore more readily absorbed by the curd.

A. Sprinkle 1 to 2 tablespoons salt over curds while they are draining and still fairly warm. Mix in well with your hand.

B. When curds are cool, taste them and add enough extra salt to flavor cheese slightly saltier than you desire finished cheese to be. Incorporate thoroughly.

HOOPING AND PRESSING

When salt dissolves and curd temperature drops (generally to 85 degrees F. unless otherwise specified in your recipe), the curds may be placed in the hoop and pressed. These are general directions. Follow recipe directions if given. (For description of equipment, *see* page 6).

STEP ONE
HOOPING

A. Drape bottom and sides of hoop with large piece of cheesecloth. Avoid bunching or any large folds.

B. Spoon in curds. Fold cheesecloth over top of curds. If cloth seems too bulky, cut it away and cover curds with a circle of cloth cut to fit top.

C. Set follower on wrapped cheese and place hoop in press. Place large plastic or glass bowl underneath to catch whey.

STEP TWO
FIRST PRESSING

A. Set weights (generally 3 or 4 bricks or other weights totaling 12 to 16 pounds) on board placed over follower. Let stand for 10 minutes.

B. Remove weights and follower and pour off any whey inside the hoop.

C. Replace hoop in press, cover with follower and board and set weights on, one every 5 minutes, until they total 25 to 30 pounds. If too much pressure is added in too short a time, the cheese will be too dry.

D. Leave full weight called for in your recipe on curds for 30 to 60 minutes.

E. Remove weights, follower and hoop from press. Turn hoop upside down on table and pull cheese from hoop.

F. Unwrap cheese and dip in warm water (100 degrees F.) to remove any surface fat.

STEP THREE
BANDAGING

A. Cut cheesecloth (or similar cotton cloth) 2 inches wider than cheese and long enough to wrap around cheese with 1-inch overlap. Turn cheese on side, and beginning at one end, roll up securely.

B. Cut two cloth circles and place on top and bottom of cheese. Return bandaged cheese to hoop, insert follower and set into press.

STEP FOUR
SECOND PRESSING

A. Increase weight, one weight at a time, to a total weight of 30 to 40 pounds (or weight called for in your recipe).

B. Let stand as directed in your recipe.

DRYING THE CHEESE

A. Remove cheese from hoop and carefully unwrap bandage. Wipe with dry cloth to remove moisture and/or butterfat from surface.

B. Inspect cheese for cracks or holes which could present entrance point for molds to attack. If there are any such imperfections, dip cheese in water to soften surface and smooth over each crack or hole with your fingers. Cut away any unevenness and make surface level.

C. Cheeses in which cracks or holes cannot be repaired in this way should be rewrapped in bandage (see Bandaging in the Hooping and Pressing section, page 72). Press again for 1 hour.

STEP TWO
DRYING

A. When cheese is free from imperfections, set in a clean, cool, moisture-free storage place for 3 to 5 days to form a rind (see Equipment List, Curing Cupboard or Shelf, page 9).

B. Dry cheese in its bandage only if it is to be coated with paraffin later on. In this case, cheese will require only 3 days' drying time.

C. If hard rind fails to develop in 6 days, your storage place may not be dry enough. Transfer cheese to drier spot for 3 days more, or until rind forms.

SEALING THE CHEESE FOR AGING

You may seal cheese either by dipping it in paraffin or by wrapping it in a plastic bag.

Before preparing the paraffin, be sure that the surface of the cheese is perfectly dry. Wax will not adhere to a moist surface. If you prefer to cure cheese in a plastic bag, see Step Three of this section.

STEP ONE
MELTING THE PARAFFIN

A. Place paraffin in pan deep enough to immerse ½ of cheese. Use old double boiler* kept especially for this purpose, since hardened paraffin is impossible to remove.

B. Melt paraffin over low heat until temperature is between 210 and 220 degrees F. Paraffin that is too cool forms too thick a coating, while overly hot paraffin covers too thinly. Paraffin may be colored before dipping, if desired.

*Note: Paraffin is highly flammable and should never be melted directly over flame.

STEP TWO
DIPPING THE CHEESE

A. Dip ½ of cheese in hot paraffin for 10 seconds. Remove and allow paraffin to cool for a few minutes.

B. Dip other ½ of cheese for 10 seconds, remove and let cool. Make sure cheese surface is completely covered before cheese is set aside to cure (age).

STEP THREE
SEALING IN A PLASTIC BAG

A. Dry cheese thoroughly, then place in plastic bag. Flatten bag closely around cheese, forcing out as much air as possible. Seal tightly.

B. Plastic bags have their drawbacks since they cannot be made perfectly airtight, but they do permit intermittent wiping of cheeses to prevent molding.

AGING, OR CURING, THE CHEESE

Once the rind has been properly hardened, paraffined or wrapped in plastic, the cheese should be returned to a cool storage place to cure (see Cheesemaking Equipment, Curing Cupboard or Shelf, page 9).

STEP ONE

A. Turn cheese once daily during first few weeks of curing to keep any seeping whey from centering in one place.

B. Scrub storage shelf once a week with soap and water, and if possible, dry in sun.

C. Cheese usually develops firm body and mild flavor within 6 weeks. Cheese flavor sharpens as it ages, so if you prefer a sharp cheese, age for 3 to 5 months (or longer). Turn cheese once a week. Cheese aged in the refrigerator takes a bit longer to ripen.

TROUBLESHOOTING

Although cheesemaking may seem a bit complicated at first, making fine cheese becomes easier each time you do it. Occasionally, however, your finished cheese may not be up to standard. Overcooking or scorching the curds is the most common reason for failure, but there are other possible causes. The quality of a finished cheese depends on several factors:

> The quality of the milk
> Proper acidity in each cheese
> Pressing the cheese sufficiently
> Correct curing techniques
> Using the proper temperatures throughout
> the entire cheesemaking process

- A sour or acid cheese is generally due to too high a level of acid in the milk or insufficient draining of the whey.
- Always use milk high in quality.
- Bitter cheese occurs when undesirable bacteria contaminate milk. Make sure your milk is always fresh and sweet.
- Sweet or fruity flavor in cheese may be caused by low-acid milk or tainted cheesemaking equipment. Make sure your equipment is spotless (see Cleanliness in Cheesemaking, page 50), and allow your cheese time enough to develop proper acidity during curdling.
- Open-textured cheeses indicate faulty pressing. Make sure curds are still fairly warm when pressed, and always apply weight called for in your recipe.
- Excess whey left in the curd gives cheese a pasty body. Firm the curd sufficiently during the cooking process.
- Improper curing heightens any defect in cheese. Always cure your cheese at temperatures below 60 degrees F.

SOURCES OF SUPPLY

- Drug stores, particularly in farm communities, often carry rennet tablets, and gourmet food shops frequently do so too. For vegetarians there is a new, all-vegetable rennet which is available in some health food stores. Try these sources before you send away for supplies.
- When tracking down cheesemaking supplies, all roads, it seems, lead to Chr. Hansen's Laboratory, Inc., 9015 W. Maple St., Milwaukee, Wisconsin 53214. Every inquiry I made was answered with "Try Chris Hansen's in Milwaukee." The firm carries rennet, cheese colors, starters, etc. They do fill individual orders and seem quite courteous over the phone.
- Another supplier whose name I have been given is American Supply House, P.O. Box 1114, Columbia, Missouri 65201.

YVONNE YOUNG TARR is a veteran cookbook writer. Her books include *The Ten Minute Gourmet Cookbook, The Ten Minute Gourmet Diet Cookbook, 101 Desserts to Make You Famous, Love Portions, The New York Times Natural Foods Dieting Book, The Complete Outdoor Cookbook, The New York Times Bread and Soup Cookbook, The Farmhouse Cookbook* and *The Up-with-Wholesome, Down-with-Storebought Book of Recipes and Household Formulas.*
She is married to sculptor William Tarr. They have two children, Jonathon and Nicolas.